The Other Myrtle

poems by

William Considine

Finishing Line Press
Georgetown, Kentucky

The Other Myrtle

To Careen

Copyright © 2021 by William Considine
ISBN 978-1-64662-394-5 First Edition
All rights reserved under International and Pan-American Copyright Conventions. No part of this book may be reproduced in any manner whatsoever without written permission from the publisher, except in the case of brief quotations embodied in critical articles and reviews.

ACKNOWLEDGMENTS

Looking to Music	Home Planet News
New Questions	Short, Fast and Deadly
Wolves	*Brownstone Poets 2019 Anthology*
Open Record	Brevitas 16.
Said Plain	Home Planet News
Dark Party	*Silver-Tongued Devil Anthology*
Myrtle	Sensitive Skin
I slumped…	White Rabbit
For the Drawer	Home Planet News
A Fantasy	Home Planet News
Jim	White Rabbit
Night Bodies	*Brownstone Poets 2018 Anthology*
An Ancient's Garden	Walt's Corner, Long Islander News
Full Moon	Home Planet News
We shared a quilt…	Home Planet News
Persephone's Return	*POSTmortem*, from Mad Gleam Press

Persephone's Return had a staged reading in the Boog City Poets Theater Festival, NYC, in September 2018. Expanded, it had a reading at Polaris North, NYC, on Zoom and YouTube in December 2020.

A Fantasy, Said Plain, An Early Spring, and Persephone's Return were read with music on the album, *An Early Spring*, from Fast Speaking Music
Looking to Music is recited by the poet in the video "21 Poets"
by John Palmer Shaw, on Vimeo.

Thank you to Ambrose Bye, Patricia Carragon, Steve Dalachinsky, Dorothy Friedman, David Kirschenbaum Craig Kite, Ron Kolm, Bernard Meisler, Frank Murphy, Joseph Quintela, John Shaw, Brian Sheffield, and George Wallace.

Publisher: Leah Huete de Maines
Editor: Christen Kincaid
Cover Art and Design: Meredith Simonds
Author Photo: Careen Shannon

Order online: www.finishinglinepress.com
also available on amazon.com

Author inquiries and mail orders:
Finishing Line Press
PO Box 1626
Georgetown, Kentucky 40324
USA

Table of Contents

Looking to Music 1
New Questions 2
Wolves 5
Critters 6
Call Home 11
All the Best 12
Open Record 13
Said Plain 14
The Falls 15
Dark Party 16
I slumped… 17
For the Drawer 18
A Fantasy 19
An Early Spring 20
Jim 22
Night Bodies 23
I Might Better 24
Myrtle 25
An Ancient's Garden 27
Green 28
Full Moon 29
Persephone's Return 30
We shared a quilt 35

Looking to Music

Washed in a hot whirlpool, bathing
chin-deep in sloshing, bubbling waters,
I look ahead through sunlight
to sonatas and trios
of intimate surprise and satisfaction.
To live long would be to hear lots of music.
To live in health would be to swim often
and rest afterward in sunshine.
And I realize how much I'm like your father,
he swam & danced & loved the same music.
After a swim, like me now, he looked forward
to see you. He too craved Saturday
afternoon radio broadcasts of opera.
While dying, he sat in his den
listening to records. He sobbed
once alone to art songs and rhapsodies,
wept for his favorite, the Rosenkavalier.
How glad I am to be too busy for much music.
I can't be distracted now from wife & child
by desire for music. If there is time,
there will be music.

New Questions

For hours in the afternoon,
we played puzzles, and my daughter
even let me watch an opera on TV
while we played.
What are they doing?
They're all singing
that they want a new king.
What happens?
A man becomes king and they sing
and then later the king dies.
I want to see the king die.

That became the day's refrain.
Is the king going to die now?
I want to see the king die.

Ten weeks ago, her Aunt Lizzie died.
Since then, at mention of Lizzie,
my daughter has turned
away and pulled inward,
her arms at her chest.

Watching the king on TV, she asks,
Will someone step on him?
(This must refer to ants
on the kitchen floor,
the first and only beings
she saw die, stepped on.)
No. He gets very sick.
Will he die on something?
He'll die on red steps. You'll see them.
People die on something.
Yes.
What did Lizzie die on?

Lizzie died sitting on a chair, dear.
This is her first mention of Lizzie
since the morning after Lizzie died.
Then she ventured to ease
her mother's grief with,
I think Lizzie's getting better now.

Is the king going to die now?
Soon, dear.
I don't see the steps.
The red steps are in front of his chair.
I want to see the king die.

The operatic climax when the great
basso Nesterenko sprawls
as dead Boris Godunov
on red stairs in the Kremlin
was my daughter's first glimpse
at age three of human dying.
She sat in my lap.

Her mother came and sat beside us
on the couch. She needed to talk
too about grief in her sister's death.
We were all pulling inward.
She answered attentively
our child's effort to share loss.

Why does he die?
He's very old, old and sick, very sick,
not a little sick like we get sometimes,
but very sick.

Why did Lizzie die?
She was very sick.
I don't like doctors,
our girl said with a shrewd look.
The doctors helped Lizzie a whole lot.
The doctors didn't make her die.
Doctors help us.

Lizzie died.
Yes, Lizzie died, and we're very sad.
I miss Lizzie.
We miss Lizzie too, very much.
Lizzie died.
Yes, she did.
But we - we won't die.

She waves among us three inclusive
loved ones, so briefly dreamed an eternity.

Her mother says,
We won't die for a long, long time.
No, I said, we won't die.
We won't die for a long, long time.
She curls her lip, looks hard
and does not dare to repeat the question,
to hear again an awful
amendment to her answer.

The next day,
I don't want to see opera again.
It's too scary.

Wolves

"When television was black-and-white,
Was everything black-and-white?"
The child asked, intrigued
By the mysterious past of parents.

From the parking lot, the little houses
Had a padlocked gate,
Like the one in Disney's cartoon
Of "Beauty and the Beast," a gate

Where a fierce pack of hungry gray wolves
Leapt to attack Belle's befuddled
Dad in the snow. From our car
To home became a frightful passage.

Dropping mother and child off at the front
Door before parking was our adult
Solution for the wolves crisis, but inside,
A spell-stricken Beast still kept Beauty captive.

Critters

1.

The cereal box
        has a huge hole.
                It's knocked over.

Cheerios, a few,
        are scattered
                But most are gone.

That's a big hole,

Too big for a mouse
        to gnaw or need,
                to get inside.

Dismiss it, a fluke.
        It cannot be.
                It's a weird anomaly.

But in the night,
        there's a skittering sound
                downstairs,

A creature of size and stealth,
        busy and bold,
                come to our house.

In the morning, stand
        in the living room.
                What's different? Where?

I stand and wait.
        It slowly comes:
                a smell.

Wet carpet? I look at my feet.
        Musk of an animal,
                Fur and raw meat...

I smell a rat.
    That's dirty flesh and fur,
        under the floor,

Under my feet,
    a rat at home, nesting
        in the joists holding up the floor,

Inches under me.
    No, not a rat.

The smell's too strong for a small creature.
    If you smell a rat,
        you're smelling lots of rats.

2.

Hardware store people are firm:
    Only glue traps will work,
        and rats need the large size.

I lay traps along the walls in the kitchen.
    Within hours, a big rat
        Is caught behind the stove,

gray and half the size of a cat,
    half-caught, crawling,
        dragging the glue-trap.

The trap bumps the stove
    and the straining rat pulls free,
        flees

fast behind the stove, gone.
    The floorboard hole for the gas pipe
        is key ground.

What sordid circumstance has brought us rats?
    Made us filthy?
        What abasement

teems with rats
        that lurk, creep, dart, steal, feed,
            escape my traps?

This disgrace is danger
        and disease,
            a threat to our young child,

big-eyed with wonder.
        "Mice" must be the word,
            never "rat."

No, "mice" is a lie,
        but "rat" must never be admitted.
            "Critters, " I say, I say

"Varmints," like Yosemite Sam. I say,
        "I'm gonna get those critters."
            But, "Dag-nab it," it got away.

3.

A neighbor also has rats suddenly.
        Just a look across the street explains it.
            There's a playground,

and to its right, a building long boarded up.
        Workmen are renovating it.
            Rats have fled from there.

In my basement I find an open window.
        My home's the exit highway
            for rats moving on

Or staying.
        I nail that window closed
            and get to work.

Glue traps are cruel, they suffer, I know.
    Glue traps are all I know.
        When a trap held a rat

Or held half a rat that dragged it,
    I'd press another glue trap
        onto its head or back

to disorient it
    and not let the rat roll out of the trap.
        I'd wait while it weakened

through struggle, hoping
    its chirps and squeaks and scrapes
        and the scent of its fear

would terrify other rats.
    Then with a shovel
        I'd thrust trapped rat squirming

into a trash bag
    and carry the bag
        to a construction dumpster.

This was no heroic hunt,
    need I tell you,
        and earned no praise.

After a big catch,
    three caught and discarded in a day,
        that night the rats went wild

in the living room.
    We could hear them from upstairs.
        They tore and toppled and dragged

candies, papers, ribbons, all sorts of little things,
    made quite a mess,
        in rage, I hope, at their loss.

4.

Glue-trapper,
   rat-grappler,
vermin-smeller,
   rat's nest dweller,
low man,
   no man,
mammal oppressor.
    Is any creature lesser?

It's a sordid secret,
   not for office talk.
     "What's new with you?"
"Rats!
   Lots of rats!
     I'm killing lots of rats in my home."

Information kept from the child,
   minimized.
     Wife averted her eyes

from the rat-man
   and his dirty duties.

As the rats ran away,
   What pulled, dragged
     me behind them?

Scraping concrete,
   no teeth tore my flesh.
     After the rats were gone,

the house emptied.
   What a mean confession
     was left.

Call Home

Outside power
charges through wires in the walls.

> O! sing open windows.
> Oh no! cry the doors.
> Hooray! rings the rooftop.
> Too late! warn the floors.

Hollow inside
is the charge against pipes.
All mine, nothing yours:
Up to code, worth a fight.

> O! sing open windows,
> Oh no! cry the doors.
> Hooray! rings the rooftop.
> Too late! warn the floors.

The house divided,
it starts to fall.
No outrage subsiding,
screams bury all.

All the Best

All the best memories
Cannot restore
Our solemn, silly and serene
Times together in
Long, now lost embrace.

Still, reflections tease me.
A touch felt more
True than months of mean
Indifference.
A fleeting smile, a taste,
Gave all of love's prodigious waste.

Open Record

While dreaming of Me,
I mostly remember you.

And what is more
Flimsy, fragile and frayed,

A couple, a thought, or
Our time gone away?

So, I open old moments to save
All that lasts of the love we gave.

Said Plain

I don't know how
Else to structure
Spontaneous effusions
As love said plain.

Do you hear now?
Within long confusions,
Across our rupture,
I sing love's refrain.

The Falls

Dark spruces whirl in the sky
on the edge of a sudden cliff.
Rock face is torn and sheer.

Down the gorge,
                white
                water
                spills
                smoothly
                down
                to drop
                straight
                into a
                pool.

      The green pool,
bottomed with brown rocks,
      always sways with impact of the falls.
          The water always sways.

      As constant as
the onrush and rocking of water
      in a gorge of a mountain,
          flows love
                for one who seems forgotten.

Dark Party

Poem begins after the dark party.
The beer in the tub poured cold as nails.
Strangers smirked in my barren study.
The music of my dance blasted the guests

To huddle in the far, dim kitchen, cold.
A chilly guest lit the oven, door open.
Neighbors spoke boldly of my shock and
Trauma. A stud-skirted woman smiled

Behind the cold friend I could not see
To the door. Some of the guests stayed
In their tiny homes and did not show
Their fear and confusion. Tight-lipped,

I paced my railroad hall. This is fun,
Drinking friends demanded. I'll throw another
Soon and a strange word will go round and round
And round: call it a success, just do it.

I slumped...

I slumped, said my laboring
friend, and slept for years
and fell accused of savoring
old adventures over beers.

People disperse
and do their own thing so fast.
I lay sick and getting worse
for years, but now that's passed.

I have an attractive girlfriend
again, that's healthy.
I'm busy again with good things.

Our old projects lend
enough for me to feel wealthy.
I'll spend what memory brings.

For the Drawer

I could not confess any faster,
In retrospect,
How proud I felt to master
Strong feelings with intellect.

It seemed a brilliant twist: I'll
Turn the form up-ended,
To finish with love's denial,
With punishing force pretended.

Then, it made ironic sense.
The form found wit in wordplay.
But after so long a silence,
Words come to mean what they say.

Not giving then, I shared no game.
To show it now would lay false blame.

A Fantasy

Those few occasions linger.
An honest desire seizes
Untouched details: her slim fingers
On a cigarette, her bare knees.
Each remembered glance
Can show she loved me.
           I made myself a lost romance.

Sometimes, I play saxophone
Through small, rapt rooms of my mind
Into hers. In a musical moan,
She knows. Meeting, we are kind
In the confusion of our eyes.
- But I never took the chance.
The unsaid dies in rich sighs.
           I made myself a lost romance.

An Early Spring

We had such a mild winter, and
Already, lunch hours are warm and sunny.
Office workers teem coatless on Lower Broadway
In mid-March, the women in dresses. I walk
North easily, and harder south, shielding my eyes
From the sun's glare straight up the Avenue,
Hat on my head, sunscreen on nose and cheeks.

Spring came so fast, I had no time to walk
In winter landscapes, to see the brown ground
Undulations. I didn't check
The place where crocus breaks the ground
In Prospect Park each year, emerging
Beyond the Boathouse, on the slope
Of the berm building up to the bridge.
It's another year I missed the crocus.

So today at lunch, I go to the tip,
The southernmost edge of Manahatta,
And turn up the Island to find more.

From Castle Clinton and the Battery north,
The cherry tree esplanade, shriven by loss,
Is hardly budding. A few magnolias splash
The land like white spray of the Harbor.
Through the bare trees, magnolias stand out.
White-tipped petals furl from bases
Lavender and pink.
To the west, the tall stand of
Maples at the entrance to Wagner Park
Has bare boughs, tipped rust-red high at the top.

On Little West Street a grand
Boulevard of forty pear trees, more,
Stands gorgeously blooming above
The entry to a tunnel, a river of cars
Pouring into the ground.

Still at the Island's tip, my back to the sea,
A crisp Empire apple in hand,
I walk past Customs,

Into the old Green, Bowling Green
At the bottom of Broadway.
Its fountain is emptied for winter.
The pathway that circles it is dusty
And clouds my shoes. The pale beige bricks
Of the fountain's pool look like parched earth,
A cracked and dry oasis. But all around
The potential fountain is a crowded ring
Of tulip bulbs. They're green and grow taller
By the day, spears of a pagan army.
Each stalk stands as a yew tree pointing to
The source, each stalk a center enfolded
In stiff leaves curling up. The green bulbs are still
Closed, but some are cracking open,
Baring lewd red lips, in a pucker, a moue,
A pout of lurid scarlet, the inner
Petals showing. Yes, the bulbs, stems and leaves
Are firm and erect, thick with water, spring's sap,
And tulip petals are pealing open
-       Blatant, rampant, growing, going wild!

Jim

This is a story I don't want to tell, so instead I'll suggest I might.

It involves a dear brother who will never appear again in this story. That was him, just now.

His name was Jim. I knew him best when we were children. I went to visit him maybe half a dozen times in the last twenty years, totaling less than three weeks. We talked on the phone, and he was always warm, good-humored, upbeat.

I'm hiding the truth: he's died.

He deserves better than a post-self, self-conscious, post-modern assemblage, but this is what he gets for dying too soon and trusting to a long-lost brother.

He had a great spirit. In long illness, he was content with life, loved his wife, children, grandchildren & friends—his two huge, frenetic dogs bounding to him, too.

There was a time he organized unions in the Rocky Mountain region. His greatest successes were with sanitation workers and clerical workers in a large city, and he settled there.

There was a time he was a State Senator, and as the only Democrat, minority leader in the State Senate.

There was a time we played in the backyard, on a swing set and with cap guns.

We ate together, so many breakfasts, lunches and dinners, and slept in matching pajamas. We ate lots of ice cream cones, Dairy Queen milk shakes, popsicles, creamsicles, drumsticks, candy cigarettes, bubble gum and great piles of Halloween loot.

Recently, for a while, he rode a motorized, seated scooter, to go to the park and watch the youth baseball leagues. The scooter was slow to cross the wide streets of his city, and those jaunts soon ended.

He used a thick walking stick, gnarled and alluding to elders as active survivors, a pillar.

He followed politics closely, a labor liberal always, with many hearty laughs.

These notes are only preliminary, as we all were.

Night Bodies

Night solves nothing.
Familiar cast
Of homegrown stars

Fail to rehearse,
Muff our lines. Scene
Staging wanders off.

Whose sprawling apartment
Is this? Mine?
The man on the couch is Dad,

Young again, but subdued.
And him - my brother Jim?
Walked in out of nowhere,

Knows maybe what happened?
Our storyline unravels.
Police have questions.

We have bodies.
We failed to cover our tracks
In time. One round

Of questioning till we're caught.
Caught what?
Conversing with the dead

Our doing,
Delving into undercurrents
Almost our undoing.

I Might Better

Reveal—for me
Hard Truth was found
In family secrets,

Sad parental moments
Reeking of booze & screams.
All I did was share—be real.

Rude Lessons—mine alone—
Grew over years to be not
What I long thought.

Insight twists—Reflection's
Pretzel cracks my front teeth. Gnaw,
Gummy—worry a bone

Over how I've coped.
What passes for Wisdom
I might better—conceal.

Myrtle

I want all the flowers
that thrive right away at the start of spring,
that stand alone in the cool noon and the long, chilly
shadows of dawn & dusk and through cold nights.

They take the first chance
opening of light & warmth, to probe out of
the hard, bare dirt, to push past the dry, dead leaves.
They poke up shoots, then leaves, then buds,
then blooms in a bustle to be.
They give the light back as life.
They brighten with the new birds that sing
on budding boughs, all the daylight hours.
They shake & shimmy with the wind,
they quiver through their quick, brisk dance.

Crocus already flared out of winter and went down.
Magnolias have bloomed and greened.
Daffodils still stretch and bob to the new music.
Now pear trees astonish the streets with
all white blossoms for one week, this week,
until the next downpour knocks their
delicacies straight down onto the pavement,
like the tree's white shadow, like one big bloom.

We find ourselves at a farmer's market
in the plaza. The crowd buzz and circle
the offerings. The sun is warm at mid-day.
Life will be better from now on. Just add flowers.
Blue hyacinths are plump as balloons,
thick and upright, fertile for sure.
Pansies flop like puppies
learning to lie down. They collapse on the ground
and lounge about, they shiver with excitement,
they roll and scamper up.

No, pansies aren't puppies. They're colorful as kites.
They shake like kites pulling on their strings,
aloft and almost carried away.
Puppies, kites, the fact is, they quiver
and look so deliciously lazy.

                        But let me show you
what's come naturally to my garden
within the last year, come on the wind
to take root. The violet is coming,
darkened, burdened with a big heart,
so to speak. Yes, the violet is returning,
the heart-shaped leaves in clusters.

                        But there are two kinds of
purple flowers here. See the paler ones, scattered
above the ivy? They bloomed before the violets.
A neighbor told me their name - periwinkle.
I'd known periwinkle only as some fashion shade,
a pastel tone, a water color. It's this,
this early, small, strewn bloom.
And it's called myrtle, too, like Myrtle Avenue
a block away. Are these surviving remnants
of the whole hill's flowering, centuries ago?
Still finding a place here? Or maybe
they've wafted from some other gardener's
homage to the past or fondness for pale myrtle.
Or maybe the hill was all another myrtle,
The flowering bush, sacred to Aphrodite.
My mistake: admiring this, the other myrtle.

Here, look closely, if you like.
Its five petals are curved, like
the air-scooping blades of a rotary fan.
The petals come together in a distinct white star,
as clear as the emblems of armies and air corps,
or the sticker on a child's first homework.
Within the star is a yellow nova halo,
the sun's horizon or the eye's iris opening,
looking back at the sun or being the blind sun.

That's all I know. I look into blossoms and see stars.
Periwinkle bursts over the ground cover ivy.
I'm shaken by the wind, but
I can look up again from the ground,
all the way up in a glance to see stars.

An Ancient's Garden

Out each latticed window is landscape
In miniature:

Pine, bamboo and banana leaf,
Planted or potted among rocks,
And a lily pond where goldfish swarm
Serve as a lake and forested hills.

Inside the study: mirrors made of marble,
Porcelain vases on rosewood shelves,
Hanging scrolls of delicate scenes and
Bold handwriting, a table as a desk:

Finally, quiet life, looking out
At limestone, artfully placed
And pock-marked with erosion,
A mountain in a corner.

Green

Gardens are repeating themselves.
Leaves unfurl in fractal elongations
of the same spiral look-alikes, green.

Light dissolves, infusing loose photons
into surface fibers, storing
energy in chloroplast batteries
of leaves, leaves, leaves.

Green wavelengths light is useless
to the process and NOT absorbed into leaves.
What we see growing everywhere
is exactly what is not essential: green.

These seasons of abundant, spectral waste,
plants spread out, filling more and more
space with energy supplies
in shapely, varied greens,
emitting fresh tastes of oxygen.

"Radiative transports!"
goes the glee of being here now,
a Cosmos down to our size, our
light in local concentration—solar.

No waste when we see!
Bonus parade: bug attractors,
showy and fragrant, bud, bloom and
pass in waves of a few weeks each,
shedding pollen and seeds.

"I give the green six months -
time enough to reproduce and then
done," said a salad-eating, oxygenated
omnivore, hydrated and soiled,
who hadn't seen it all,
just enough to sense what air and light allotted.

Cycling out of relapse fills our comfort zone:
easy enough to rest and open out again.

Full Moon

The full white moon,
drunk with so many
memories of love,
twists its round mouth
and howls a loony tune.

"O humans of the dark
blue planet, facing skies!
Your small white eyes
gleam like so many
stars radiating into stark,
near nothing space
a faded Being's final trace.
The light returning from your eyes
is fire of the love
God left at your thighs."

Sky-gazing men and women,
seduced through the open
moaning of the moon
—"O!" says the big face
in a cosmic cartoon—
feel touched by grace
implicit in our sense of place.

Hugging old confusions
as our own dear conclusions,
spinning dizzy dreams
in dim and mixed-up scenes,
jilted, faithful lovers croon
for shadows on our bright balloon.

Persephone's Return
For Diane Middlebrook

Cast: Female: the goddesses Hera, Athena, Demeter and Persephone
         Male: the god Zeus

Athena is onstage. Hera enters.

Hera: There's been a catastrophe.
A girl has been taken.
None of us are free of what will follow.

Athena: Who?

Hera: Persephone, daughter of Demeter.

Athena: Persephone! So young and innocent.
Demeter scorned the men who wanted her.
She kept the girl well-protected.

Hera: She lingered in fields, gathering flowers.
Out of the earth, Hades rode a stallion up
And snatched her. Draped across his saddle,
Under his arm, he carried her off.

Athena: Hades - Lord of Death!

Hera: Demeter is in a rage, scorching
The earth that hides both crime and daughter.
The crops are burned. Hunger will be brutal.

Demeter enters.

Hera: Dear! Demeter! How awful!

Athena: How can we help?

Demeter: Zeus must get her back. It's his brother!
Persephone is Zeus's daughter,
Taken like a simple slave!
He cannot have her torn from me
To live in shadows and darkness.
I'll get her back.

Athena:	You will!
All:	She will return!
Demeter:	Where is the foremost of the gods?
Athena:	The old bull, the goat, the swan, The master of misleading?
Hera:	He was pacing an empty palace.
Demeter:	Is he frantic for his daughter?
Hera:	More, he misses the savor of Roasted offerings in prayer. You've turned people from the gods. Without their regard, we're nothing.
Demeter:	My first prayer is for my child.

Enter Zeus.

Zeus:	It is a terrible thing, to take a child.
Demeter:	She's your own child, Lightning Hurler.
Zeus:	And I gave her to Hades, in marriage. He reached for her with love. He loves her.
Demeter:	You took her from me.
Zeus:	You were too protective. We never Could have made this match with you hovering.
Demeter:	And she's taken from me forever?
Zeus:	No. As we once agreed to slumber And renew, slumber and renew, We can agree now together.
Athena:	Agree to what?

Zeus: Agree to my brother as the girl's good husband.
He's as worthy as me. He just drew
The world of death as his domain,
A hard fate, and he needs the girl's comfort.
I approved and he acted swiftly.
Be gracious as your hopes and make this good:
Our daughter queen among the strongest gods.

Demeter: Accept the waste of all the sunlit world,
All your river nymphs parched and dry,
The maidens weak with hunger - a hard fate
for you, to be barren of worship.

Zeus: I see in you the hurt I've caused you.
I went too far. I can't deny you
And all we were together.
I'll make this right with you.

Demeter: You will at once.

Zeus: So now I must take the girl,
Back from a loving husband, take her
Back from my brother.
I promised her to him. He longs for her.
This may be fatal. You'll have me cross him?

Demeter: Your rash actions may be fatal to the gods.

Zeus: But all depends on this: she cannot have eaten
in the long night of death. The fruit of twilight
tastes eternal. It seems to satisfy.
It tempts but holds and never lets go.
No one comes back.

Athena: Who's coming now? Can it be?

Persephone enters.

Persephone: Mother!

Demeter: Persephone!

Hera: You're back with us!

Athena: We love you!

Persephone: But I've completely changed.

Zeus: Persephone is now a queen.

Persephone: As my mother is enamored of the earth,
I now enjoy the comforts smothered within
My daily engagement to death.
He rules multitudes and so many more arriving.
All of them wander in silence, musing
On their distant pasts and parents,
As if all that happened then is still now.
All they see is that distance to what's gone.

Athena: All of them? All of them feel the same?

Persephone: They're just as I imagine them, so yes,
All the dead are soon the same,
When there's no one left to love them still,
and that comes for all, a second death.

Hera: But who is left to know?

Persephone: You will know, because now I've told you.

Demeter: You may return among the living, you're free.

Persephone: But I have tasted power over death and
so I'm perverted past this life's mild spice
of the fleeting and their fast departures,
their nervous numbering of decline.
I snack on seeds of pomegranate
Gathered in death's vast dominion.
I bite to burst the bulbs of nectar.
I grind the seeds to toughen teeth and bones.
Seven seeds are just a beginning.

Demeter: So you 're lost to me?

Persephone: For half the year, I will
rule in hell. For half the year,
we'll live together still.

Demeter: So it will be. And with you all the world
will cycle and change. The earth will lie
cold in stark shadows or dim while you're gone.

Hera: Then let the land bloom with her return.
Please let us share in your joy with her.

Demeter: Yes, gladly.

Persephone: Gladly.

Athena: Sing we still of flowers and corn silks.

Hera: Sing we still while berries are ripe.

- after Ovid's *Metamorphoses*, Book V
translated by Rolf Humphries

We shared a quilt…
    After Ts'ao Chih

We shared a quilt,
a lightweight summer quilt
made of silk, soft and smooth.
It draped our embraces, flowed
over every contour.
An open window
let a breeze pass over us.

By late September,
the quilt was too light,
air cold, wind turning
blustery and harsh.

A cotton comforter
covered us with bulk and
weight, a bulwark against
airborne elements,
our envelope,
our slot we fit within.

For a few weeks,
we kept the window open
a crack,
then closed it tight.

Under a heavier quilt,
we lay together to sleep
close all the nights of
months through winter.

When you must go
again to the border
problems or beyond,
our quilts are still here,
ready for your return.

William Considine was born in McKeesport. PA. His father was a fireman, with a sideline as a plumber. He first worked to assist his father in the plumbing. He obtained higher education on scholarships and work-study. He graduated "With Great Distinction" from Stanford and cum laude from Harvard Law School. He was first encouraged to write poetry by Diane Middlebrook at Stanford and first formally studied writing poetry at Harvard with Elizabeth Bishop.

Bill was a member of the playwrights workshop of the New York Shakespeare Festival Public Theater, coordinated by Ed Bullins, with four staged readings there. He had play performances at Theater for the New City, La Mama, the Brooklyn Army Terminal, Limbo Lounge, Ear Inn, ABC No Rio and Dixon Place. He was active in the downtown NYC poetry world in the 1980's, published in journals and featured at numerous poetry venues. He also made poetry videos. His video of his long poem "Lincoln in Queens" won the Hometown USA Award from the National Federation of Local Cable Programmers in 1990, for excellence in video art produced on public access facilities.

He had a long hiatus from creative work, returning to it in 2011.

A volume of his produced, verse plays, *The Furies*, was published by The Operating System in 2017. A chapbook of poems, *Strange Coherence*, was published in 2013 by The Operating System. A CD of poems with music, *An Early Spring*, was released by Fast Speaking Music in 2013. His full-length, family drama *Moral Support* had its premiere production at Medicine Show Theatre in February 2019, to critical praise. His full-length verse play *Women's Mysteries*, concerning Solon the Lawgiver and the Delphic and Eleusinian mysteries, had a staged reading at Polaris North, NYC in June 2019. He is a member of the Dramatists Guild, the Polaris North theater artists cooperative, and Brevitas, a poets' cooperative.

In his legal career, he served as a Lecturer in Law at Pace Law School, as an administrative law judge for the City of New York, as an arbitrator of insurance disputes, and as a senior lawyer and manager for a New York City municipal agency and for a public service corporation for dispute resolution. As *pro bono* counsel for two community boards, he negotiated in 2000 the re-establishment of Canal Park, a two-thirds acre site in Manhattan that had been designed by Calvert Vaux and Samuel Parsons Jr. The park had been destroyed in construction of the Holland Tunnel and had remained a paved storage area overlaying substantial utility conduits for almost 80 years. Re-designed and planted, Canal Park re-opened in 2005.

He retired as a lawyer in 2016 and lives in Brooklyn with his wife.

For more, please see his website at *www.williamconsidine.com*.

www.ingramcontent.com/pod-product-compliance
Lightning Source LLC
LaVergne TN
LVHW041558070426
835507LV00011B/1159